Pebble® Plus

Places in Our Community

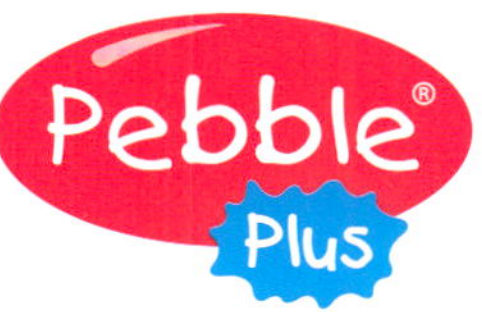

Our Farmers' Market

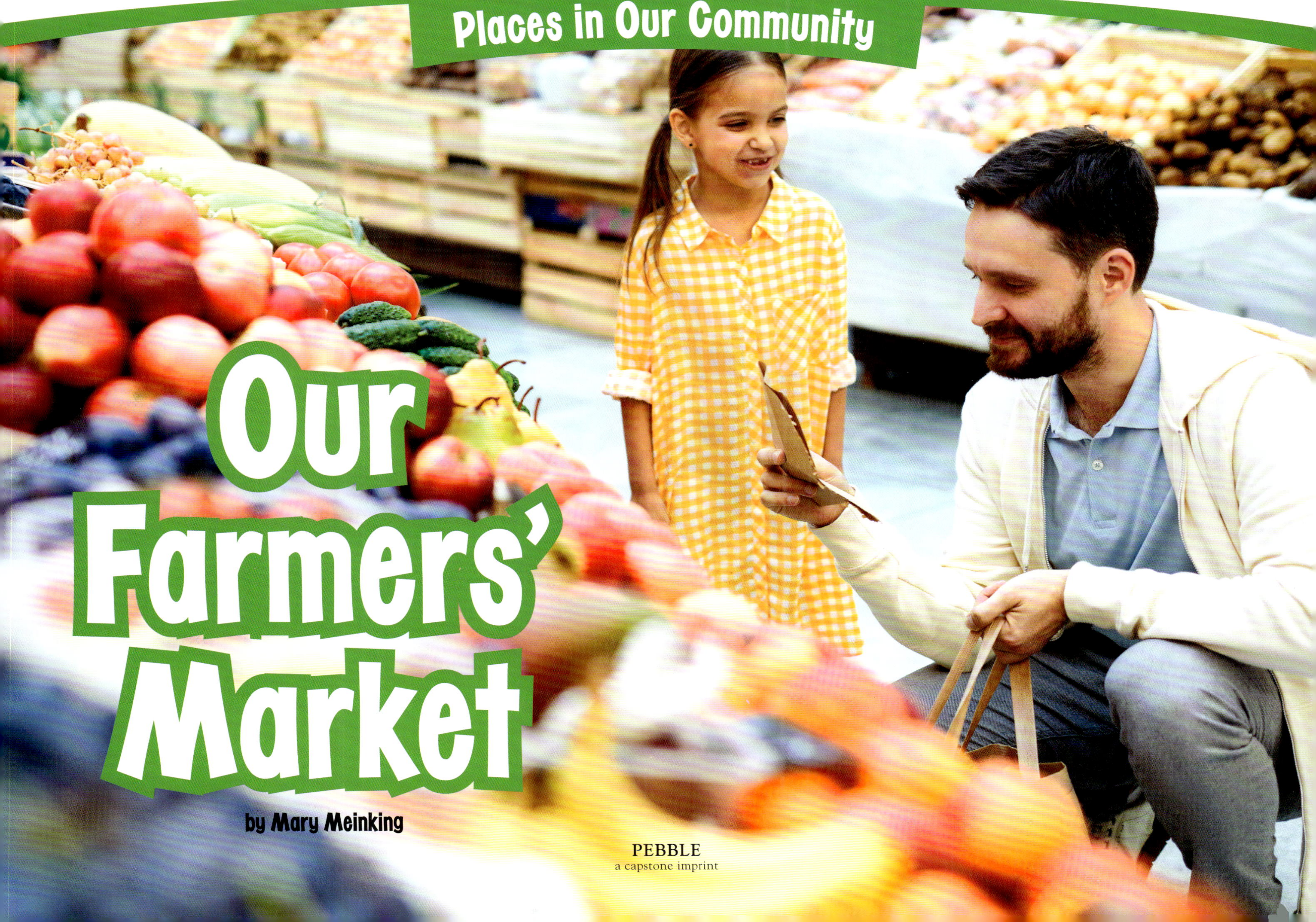

by Mary Meinking

PEBBLE
a capstone imprint

Pebble Plus is published by Pebble an imprint of Capstone
1710 Roe Crest Drive, North Mankato, Minnesota 56003
www.capstonepub.com

Library of Congress cataloging-in-publication data is available of the Library of Congress website.
ISBN 978-1-9771-1260-6 (library binding)
ISBN 978-1-9771-1767-0 (paperback)
ISBN 978-1-9771-1266-8 (eBook PDF)

Summary: Our farmers' market is a busy place! Lots of community helpers work at the farmers' market. Readers will learn about who works at a farmers' market, what the workers do, and what makes a farmers' market special. Simple, at-level text and vibrant photos help readers learn all about farmers' markets in the community.

Editorial Credits
Editor: Mari Schuh; Designers: Kay Fraser and Ashlee Suker; Media Researcher: Eric Gohl;
Production Specialist: Katy LaVigne

Photo Credits
iStockphoto: FatCamera, 19, Jayson_lys, 5, kali9, 13; Newscom: ZUMA Press/Renee Jones Schneider, 11; Shutterstock: Alexxndr, 2 (notebooks), Betelgejze, 3, Daniel Jedzura, 4, 6, 8, 10, 12, 14, 16, 18, 20, DW labs Incorporated, 22, Elena Elisseeva, 23, Matej Kastelic, 2 (vegetables), Monkey Business Images, cover, 21, 24, Pressmaster, 1, Rawpixel.com, 7, 17, riekephotos, 15, RomarioIen, back cover, YuG, 9

Note to Parents and Teachers

The Places in Our Community set supports national social studies standards related to people, places, and environments. This book describes and illustrates a farmers' market and the people who work there. The images support early readers in understanding the text. The repetition of words and phrases helps early readers learn new words. This book also introduces early readers to subject-specific vocabulary words, which are defined in the Glossary section. Early readers may need assistance to read some words and to use the Table of Contents, Glossary, Read More, Internet Sites, Critical Thinking Questions, and Index sections of the book.

All internet sites appearing in back matter were available and accurate when this book was sent to press.

Printed and bound in China.
002493

Table of Contents

Let's Visit a Farmers' Market!

Look at that rainbow of food!

This is a farmers' market.

It is filled with fresh vegetables.

There are breads and crafts too.

Let's find out more!

Who Works at a Farmers' Market?

Vendors work at
the farmers' market.
They grow and sell fruits
and vegetables. Others sell
honey, eggs, or meat.

ORGANIC
EGG
$3 99
DOZEN
MARKET
FRESH
RADISH
$2 10

What smells so good?
Bakers sell breads and desserts
at the market. Others sell jelly
or canned food. People also sell
crafts, jewelry, or pottery.

A market manager is in charge
of the farmers' market. She tells
vendors where to set up and
sell items. She advertises so
shoppers can find the market.

MAPLE GROVE
FARMERS MARKET
Thursdays
3:00 p.m. - 7:00 p.m.
Mid June - Late October
Maple Grove Community Center

What Workers Do

It is time to get ready!

Vendors get to the market early.

They set up tables, canopies, and signs. Then they set out items to sell.

$2.00
BASKET
- YELLOW SQUASH
ZUCHINNI   - EGGPLANT
PEPPERS   - TOMATOES
- RED POTATOES   - BEETS
- TOMATOES
- Sweet Potatoes
ETC

Vendors often weigh the food they sell. Then they bag the items. They put their money into a cashbox. Some vendors give away samples and recipes.

Vendors put out more items during the day. When the market ends, everything is boxed up. Some food is given to people in need.

FRESH PRODUCE
LOC LY GROWN
MER S
RKET
FRUITS & VEGETABLES
FRESH EGGS
MEATS & CHEESE
BREADS & PRESERVES
100
ORGANIC
LEMON
99 ¢
EACH
BEETROOT
4 00 LB
ESH
ADISH
3 10 LB
100% ORGANIC
17

Fresh Food!

Supermarkets sell food that comes from far away. Farmers' markets are different. They sell food that's grown nearby. The food is very fresh!

to our FARM

At farmers' markets, shoppers
learn who grew or baked
the food. They try new food
and meet people. Farmers'
markets bring people together!

Glossary

advertise—to give information about something you want to sell

crafts—items made by hand

pottery—pots, vases, dishes, and other items that are made from clay

supermarket—a large store that sells food and other items

vendor—a person who grows and sells something

Read More

Dinmont, Kerry. *Alex Eats the Rainbow: A Book About Healthy Eating.* North Mankato, MN: Child's World, 2017.

Lindeen, Mary. *A Visit to the Market.* Chicago: Norwood House Press, 2016.

Reader, Jack. *A Trip to the Farmers' Market.* New York: PowerKids Press, 2017.

Rustad, Martha E.H. *Yellow Foods.* North Mankato, MN: Capstone Press, 2017.

Internet Sites

Farmer's Market Create-and-Play Activity Book
https://www.storey.com/wp-content/uploads/2017/05/
FarmersMarket-MarketHandout-VF.pdf

American Farm Bureau: Farmers Market Challenge
http://www.myamericanfarm.org/classroom/games

How to Eat a Rainbow: A Healthy Eating Game
https://www.famlii.com/play-eat-a-rainbow-game-healthy-
eating-rules-printable-game-board/

Critical Thinking Questions

1. Name three items that are often sold at farmers' markets.

2. How is a farmers' market different from a supermarket?

3. Why might farmers' markets be popular places to buy food?

Index